WORD FOR WORD

Poetry by Matthew Mead

Word for Word

SELECTED TRANSLATIONS
FROM GERMAN POETS

Ruth and Matthew Mead

ANVIL PRESS POETRY

Published in 2009
by Anvil Press Poetry Ltd
Neptune House 70 Royal Hill London SE10 8RF
www.anvilpresspoetry.com

This book is published with financial assistance
from Arts Council England

Designed and set in Monotype Bembo by Anvil
Printed and bound in England
by Cromwell Press Group
Trowbridge, Wiltshire

ISBN 978 0 85646 405 8

A catalogue record for this book
is available from the British Library

For Malcolm Rutherford

Contents

Urs Oberlin

H. C. Artmann

Heinz Winfried Sabais

Introduction

MY WIFE and I became translators by chance if not by accident. In 1962 we were sitting quite comfortably in Bad Godesberg when a friend, back from a visit to her native Leipzig, brought us a copy of the 1961 East German edition of *Sarmatische Zeit* by Johannes Bobrowski. The small book was bound in black. There was no dust wrapper and no blurb. The title and the author's name were in red letters on the black background and the book had a loose cover of transparent plastic which carried with it the faint suggestion of celluloid. 'This is the chap they are all talking about' said my wife. I was an unknown poet trying to learn German. I had never actually read anything by a socialist poet who lived in a socialist country. I opened the book. I could understand words. I could make out some sentences. 'I can't understand it' I said to my wife. 'Would it be possible to see what one poem says, in English?' She nodded. Our greatest asset was her English which was only slightly worse than mine. With that asset in play I wrote:

> *Call*
>
> Vilna, you
> oak –
> my birch,
> Novgorod –
> once in the woods the cry
> of my springs flew up, my days'
> step sounded across the river ...

We had made a start. Details of how we continued are in my 'Translating Bobrowski' (Contemporary Authors Autobiography Series, Vol. 15, Gale Research Inc, Detroit, USA, 1991).

This selection of translations, *Word for Word*, is of poetry written in the latter part of the twentieth century by poets who had reached maturity by that time. All the German poets here – there are two Austrians and one Swiss – will have been influenced by the experience of their country: the lost war and the loss of the East; the division of the Germany which remained into the capitalist West (BRD) and the Communist East (DDR); and the Soviet-style dictatorship in the East. Three poets in particular seem to have encountered the experience in their own persons. They are Johannes Bobrowski, Heinz Winfried Sabais and Horst Bienek.

The chief concern of Bobrowski's poetry is for the land of lost content, a land in his case of an enormous size, which he called Sarmatia; a land known, to Roman historians, a country of nomads stretching from the Vistula and the Danube to the Volga and the Caucasus, an empire founded in 400 BC and overthrown centuries later by the Goths. Beyond it lay Russia which Bobrowski knew as a soldier and a long-serving prisoner of war. The attraction of Bobrowski's poetry for his German audience was said to be its 'Eastern-ness'.

Sabais's poem 'Generation' centres on his experience as a war-time pilot and the negations which he found both in the DDR, from which he fled 'with life and limb in danger', and in the BRD. 'Generation' was the first poem by Sabais which we translated, in 1966. Translating Sabais's poems with my wife over the years I was on occasion surprised to find myself writing down things which, even allowing for the ventriloquist's-dummy aspect of translation, I might have written myself.

Horst Bienek was arrested at the age of 21 on a political charge in East Berlin and sentenced to twenty-five years' forced labour of which he served four years in the prison camp of Vorkuta in Russia. Released by an amnesty he came to the West. His writings tell the tale.

Nelly Sachs escaped from Nazi Germany in 1940.

I make the above points because I am sometimes asked how like or unlike are German and English poetry. This is a question I am not qualified to answer but I think some of the difference could be explained by these German poets' experiences for which I know of no English equivalents. Anyone wishing to compare German poems in translation with English poems might set some of the work of Christa Reinig beside that of Wendy Cope. The trick will be to listen for the echoes from one lady to the other. Less productive, but perhaps as interesting, would be to place the poems in Christian Geissler's *songs from the old folk's home* beside Philip Larkin's poem 'The Old Fools' (in *High Windows*).

I have met in the flesh only two of the poets here, Wolfgang Bächler, apparently fresh from a party, on a rainy evening in Bad Godesberg, and Heinz Winfried Sabais in Darmstadt, the city of which he became Oberburgermeister. I heard H. C. Artmann read in Vienna at the only poetry-reading I have ever attended anywhere.

The ability of a German-speaking poet to 'make it new' will be found in Artmann's 'Persian Quatrains'. The Fitzgerald–Omar quatrain was so 'worn out' as to be of almost no current use except as Pound used it in Canto LXXX, for a special effect; and Pound's effect is, in intent, nostalgically 'historic'. Artmann takes the form and with a technical genius of lengthened lines and varied pauses makes something that does not lull us to sleep with its regularity after a few stanzas, his innovations have made viable again a form in which he has written some of the tenderest love poems of our time.

The poets in *Word for Word* are not the only poets we have translated but they are the only poets we have published in book or pamphlet form. And there were yet

other poets in whose work we met the rock of untrans-
latability on which our efforts floundered. We hope that
what we have been able to do will bridge some gaps
between the languages.

RMM

2007

Nelly Sachs

A Dead Child Speaks

My mother held me by my hand.
Then someone raised the knife of parting:
So that it should not strike me,
My mother loosed her hand from mine.
But she lightly touched my thighs once more
And her hand was bleeding –

After that the knife of parting
Cut in two each bite I swallowed –
It rose before me with the sun at dawn
And began to sharpen itself in my eyes –
Wind and water ground in my ear
And every voice of comfort pierced my heart –

As I was led to death
I still felt in the last moment
The unsheathing of the great knife of parting.

If I Only Knew

If I only knew
On what your last look rested.
Was it a stone that had drunk
So many last looks that they fell
Blindly upon its blindness?

Or was it earth,
Enough to fill a shoe,
And black already
With so much parting
And with so much killing?

Or was it your last road
That brought you a farewell from all the roads
You had walked?

A puddle, a bit of shining metal,
Perhaps the buckle of your enemy's belt,
Or some other small augury
Of heaven?

Or did this earth,
Which lets no one depart unloved,
Send you a bird-sign through the air,
Reminding your soul that it quivered
In the torment of its burnt body?

Chorus of the Stones

We stones
When someone lifts us
He lifts the Foretime –
'When someone lifts us
He lifts the Garden of Eden –
When someone lifts us
He lifts the knowledge of Adam and Eve
And the serpent's dust-eating seduction.

When someone lifts us
He lifts in his hand millions of memories
Which do not dissolve in blood
Like evening.
For we are memorial stones
Embracing all dying.

We are a satchel full of lived life.
Whoever lifts us lifts the hardened graves of earth.
You heads of Jacob,
For you we hide the roots of dreams
And let the airy angels' ladders
Sprout like the tendrils of a bed of bindweed.

When someone touches us
He touches the wailing wall.
Like a diamond your lament cuts our hardness
Until it crumbles and becomes a soft heart –
While you turn to stone.
When someone touches us
He touches the forked ways of midnight
Sounding with birth and death.

When someone throws us –
He throws the Garden of Eden –
The wine of the stars –
The eyes of the lovers and all betrayal –

When someone throws us in anger
He throws aeons of broken hearts
And silken butterflies.

Beware, beware
Of throwing a stone in anger –
Breath once transfused our minglement,
Which grew solid in secret
But can awaken at a kiss.

Chorus of the Unborn

We the unborn
The yearning has begun to plague us
The shores of blood broaden to receive us
Like dew we sink into love
But still the shadows of time lie like questions
Over our secret.

You who love,
You who yearn,
Listen, you who are sick with parting:
We are those who begin to live in your glances,
In your hands which are searching the blue air
We are those who smell of morning.
Already your breath is inhaling us,
Drawing us down into your sleep
Into the dreams which are our earth
Where night, our black nurse,
Lets us grow
Until we mirror ourselves in your eyes
Until we speak into your ear.

We are caught
Like butterflies by the sentries of your yearning –
Like birdsong sold to earth –
We who smell of morning,
We future lights for your sorrow.

Israel

Israel,
more nameless then,
still ensnared in the ivy of death,
in you eternity worked secretly, dream-deep
you mounted
the enchanted spiral of the moon towers,
circling the constellations disguised
by animal masks –
in the mute miraculous silence of Pisces
or the battering charges of Aries.

Until the sealed sky broke open
and you,
most daredevil of sleepwalkers,
fell, struck by the wound of God
into the abyss of light –

Israel,
zenith of longing,
wonder is heaped
like a storm upon your head,
breaks in your time's mountains of pain.

Israel,
tender at first, like the song of a bird
and the talk of suffering children
the source of the living God,
a native spring,
flows from your blood.

Butterfly

What lovely aftermath
is painted in your dust.
You were led through the flaming
core of earth,
through its stony shell,
webs of farewell in the transient measure.

Butterfly
blessed night of all beings!
The weights of life and death
sink down with your wings
on the rose
which withers with the light ripening homewards.

What lovely aftermath
is painted in your dust.
What royal sign
in the secret of the air.

In the Blue Distance

In the blue distance
where the red row of apple trees wanders
– rooted feet climbing the sky –
the longing is distilled
for all those who live in the valley.

The sun, lying by the roadside
with magic wands,
commands the travellers to halt.

They stand still
in the glassy nightmare
while the cricket scratches softly
at the invisible

and the stone dancing
changes its dust to music.

Fleeing

Fleeing,
what a great reception
on the way –

Wrapped
in the wind's shawl
feet in the prayer of sand
which can never say amen
compelled
from fin to wing
and further –

The sick butterfly
will soon learn again of the sea –
This stone
with the fly's inscription
gave itself into my hand –

I hold instead of a homeland
the metamorphoses of the world –

Thus the Mountain Climbs

Thus the mountain climbs
into my window.
Love is inhuman,
transports my heart
into the splendour of your dust.
My blood becomes a melancholy granite.
Love is inhuman.

Night and death build their land
inwards and outwards –
not for the sun.
Star is a sealed evening word –
ripped
by the inhuman upsurge
of love.

Max Hölzer

Another genesis
Mountain-range of Krokmo
the taste of north and winter
retransmuted

A dead mare lies under the snow
the tongue
is heavy
beheaded pine-trees
in the circus of cloud
the pole wakes the rubble

Not a word broke the silence
man and woman lay in unfathomed depth
they opened eyes and lips
two kinds of flesh in the bright wind

The hangman was invisible
liquid with fear what welled
from their entwining:

A sea froze
as they fled from each other.

'FLOWERS OF OUR ANATOMY ...'

Flowers of our anatomy
dance in the sky

in the ice-coffin of the lake
the skeleton sits up

Don Quixote rides
through the bed of the glacier

in his eye-sockets
lies red snow.

'WHAT WE NO LONGER SEE WITH THE EYES ...'

What we no longer see with the eyes
has died
What unmoving air
bears in its womb
our embraces

In the mirror
is no one
or others

How could we not have believed
as we
returned
once again
that a forest stood

What had we forgotten

Face to face
we saw the others
whom we were
in the mirror which quite forgot us

We with our embraces
also
died
Our memory is not so real
as the memory
of a photograph

What we no longer see with the eyes
is dead
Only we ourselves
go on dying
with the remembrance.

She is the queen
The white source reached to the heart
Into the hips enclosed in our arms
streamed all the memory
we have of earth
Wrath and revenge her offspring on the horizon

And he said of the role
of Clytemnestra:
naked
she should be played naked
that astonishment curb our fear
and we be justified and know
when we, lead past her bier
before we ourselves are killed,
see the dead woman clothed.

Woman and Bird

The grass does not penetrate the pores
of the white body
in the field
where a raven waits big as a bush
the grass burns in the sky

After the wind scrubs the roofs
clean with the ash
of the tilers
the grass burns
like a sun
in the sky
to gild the earth for the woman

A crack in the dry ground

Split in the bird's beak

None of the lightnings
with which the vastness hunts, itself
strikes into her
her eyes are empty

The white of the thighs is set in coal
Past and future have blackened
in mass of hair
A long bird-foot descends
steps over the wall of day

She is hurled
from the tower of light

she is hurled again and again
She pours herself like abundance
there on the bare earth
bright and stiff and the thighs spread
Above her the ostrich-head
stares into space

The high moment is like the crucifixion of a slave
There is no feeling
for the reality of the crucifixion
Slaves are as stiff as sticks
and do not distinguish when they eat
between the bread of love and the bread of death

Under a sky of iridescent feathers
the nerves of bread tremble

She who sat
in the field
her soul mounted in flame
her shell-white body
in this
day
crystal become flesh
softening
admitting death

Her nakedness
is a wall of wishes

What huge bird of iron and air
vibrates
in the detachment of awaking

Her body is
like the holy sepulchre
courted by black fragments

Johannes Bobrowski

The Sarmatian Plain

Soul,
full of darkness, late –
the day with open
pulses, azure –
the plain sings.

Her
song, who
bound to the coast
repeats her swaying song:
sea after storm
her song –

But the towns hear you
– white, quiet
with old sounds –
listen for you on the banks.
Your airs come to them
with a heavy smell
like sand.

And the villages are yours.
The narrow roads run
to you on the greening earth,
on the burnt-out site of your summers
is laid the ashen track
– glass powdered from tears.

There the cattle go,
breathing softly before

the dark. And a child
follows them
piping; the old woman
calls after him
from the fence.

Plain,
gigantic sleep
huge with dreams, your sky
wide, a bell-tower,
the larks high
in the vault –

Rivers along your flanks,
the wet shadows
of the woods, the bright
unending fields,

there the people
whom you preserved
from darkness trod out
their endless time
on the routes of birds
in the early year. I see you:
the heavy beauty
of the blind clay head
– Ischtar or some other name –
found in the mud.

Fishingport

At evening
before the boats go
out, one after the other,
then I love you.

Until the morning
I love you with straw in the chamber,
with the land-wind over the roof,
with the hedge before your house,
with the dogs barking
before it is light.

My face tainted with fish, in dew
I shall come, one
whose hot hands
squander warmth on the silver form of
night. Here he comes
with his salty mouth. Now
he jumps into the last boat.

The Road of the Armies

Aloof on the broken road,
in the crows' tracks on the snow,
drove the Corsican, a southern emperor,
shrunken with anger, –
overtaken at evening
by holy curses. The hungry
wolves dragged nights
of marsh-haze after him.

Yet the blue autumn
reaches for village and cloud.
Now, paths of home,
your beauty is like tears.
Sandy paths, the years
have stepped you out.

Years, tree-breaking winters,
when we listened for the light,
singing over the fire;
leant hard on the rock
of darkness and looked
for the dancing islands of the southern seas.

And we thirst.
Thus your heart, home,
has become a well
for us, smelled
in the sap of birches,
in the ferny golden nest
of your snakes.

Thus have your sons
with shadowy eyes
always returned to love
from foreign tables. –

Once,
here on the dark slope,
Orpheus walked. The wood
resounds eternally
with his lament.

Ah, the earth fooled
the singer; the many-voiced
Eurydice, from ravine,
from waters. She bows
our backs deeper in the
dank weed, before the year
goes out, with showers,
with angry rain.

Dead Language

He with the beating wings
outside who brushes the door,
that is your brother, you hear him.
Laurio he says, water,
a bow, colourless, deep.

He came down with the river,
drifting around mussel
and snail, spread like a fan
on the sand and was green.

Warne he says and *wittan*,
the crow has no tree,
I have the power to kiss you,
I dwell in your ear.

Tell him you do not
want to listen –
he comes, an otter, he comes
swarming like hornets, he cries,
a cricket, he grows with the marsh
under your house, he whispers
in the well, *smordis* you hear,
your black alder will wither,
and die at the fence tomorrow.

Pruzzian Elegy

To sing you
one song,
bright with angry love –
but dark, bitter with
grieving, like wet meadow-
herbs, like the bare pines
on the cliff, groaning
beneath the pale dawn wind,
burning before evening –

your never sung
fall, which struck us once
in the blood as our days
of child's-play hung
dream-wide –

then in the forests of the homeland,
above the green sea's
foaming impact, we shuddered
where groves had smoked
with sacrifice, before stones,
by long sunken-in gravemounds,
grass-grown ramparts, under the linden
lightly bent with age –

how rumour hung in its branches!
So in the old women's songs
sounds yet
the scarcely to be fathomed
call of the Foretime –
how we heard then

the echo rotting, the cloudy
discoloured sediment!
So when the deep bells
break, a cracked
tinkle remains.

People of the black woods,
of heavy thrusting rivers,
of empty Haffs, of the sea!
People
of the night-hunt,
of the herds and summer fields!
People
of Perkun and Pikoll,
of the corn-crowned Patrimpe!
People,
like no other, of joy!
People,
like no other, no other, of death! –

People
of smouldering groves,
of burning huts, green corn
trampled, blood-stained rivers –
People,
sacrificed to the singeing
lightning-stroke; your cries veiled
by clouds of flame –
People,
leaping before the strange
god's mother in the throat-
rasping dance
and falling –
how she precedes her

armoured might, rising
above the forest! how the Son's
gallows follows her! –

Names speak of
a stamped-out people, hillsides,
rivers, often still lustreless,
stones and roads –
songs in the evening and legends,
the rustle of lizards names you
and today, like water in the marsh,
a song, poor
with grieving –

poor like the catch of that
white-haired fisherman, always there
on the Haff when the sun
goes down.

Lake Ilmen 1941

Wilderness. Against the wind.
Numb. The river sunk
into the sand.
Charred branches:
the village before the clearing. Then
we saw the lake –

– Days of the lake. Of light.
A track in the grass,
the white tower stands
like a gravestone
deserted by the dead.
The broken roof
in the caw of crows.
– Nights of the lake. The forest
falls into the marshes.
The old wolf,
fat from the burnt-out site,
startled by a phantom.
– Years of the lake. The armoured
flood. The climbing darkness
of the waters. One day
it will strike
the storming birds from the sky.

Did you see the sail? Fire
stood in the distance. The
wolf crossed the clearing.
Listens for the bells of winter.
Howls for the enormous
cloud of snow.

Kaunas 1941

Town,
branches over the river,
copper-coloured, like branching candles.
The banks call from the deep.
Then the lame girl
walked before dusk,
her skirt of darkest red.

And I know the steps,
the slope, this house. There is no
fire. Under this roof
lives the Jewess, lives whispering
in the Jews' silence
– the faces of the daughters
a white water. Noisily
the murderers pass the gate. We walk
softly, in musty air, in the track of wolves.

At evening we looked out
over a stony valley. The hawk
swept round the broad dome.
We saw the old town, house after house
running down to the river.

Will you walk over
the hill? The grey processions
– old men and sometimes boys –
die there. They walk
up the slope ahead of the slavering wolves.

Did my eyes avoid yours
brother? Sleep struck us
at the bloody wall. So we went on
blind to everything. We looked
like gipsies at the villages
in the oak-wood, the summer
snow on the roofs.

I shall walk on the stone banks
under the rainy bushes,
listen in the haze of the plains.
There were swallows upstream
and the woodpigeon called
in the green night:
My dark is already come.

Return

Bench, a hard meuble.
There, between pine-trees,
the swing – a board, two rough
poles. Cuckoo,
blue roller and hoopoe;
the nightingale, thrush-nightingale,
sings shorter, laconically,
huskier, God willing.

But I came to sleep
under the log-wall,
sleep of gossamer and toad's gold,
fly-legged sleep. The light
recedes. Cows plod
in their own shadows. The fish
strikes a foaming line
across the water.

But I only sleep.
I am not here.
I seek a place,
only a grave wide, the little hill
over the meadows. From there
I can see
the river.

One Day

One day we shall have
both hands full of light –
the strophes of night, the moving
waters meeting the banks
again, the rough eyeless
sleep of the beasts in the reeds
after the embrace – then
we shall stand against the slope,
outside, against the white
sky which comes cold
over the hill, the cascade of radiance,
and is frozen, ice,
as if fallen from stars.

I want to rest for that
little while upon your brow,
forgetful, letting
my blood wander silent
through your heart.

The Memel

Beyond the fields, far,
beyond the meadows,
the river.
From its breath
the night rises.
The bird crosses the hill
and cries.

Once we went
with the wind, fixed the net
at the mouth of the meadowbrook.
A lantern hung
in the alders. The old man
took it down.
The smugglers' boat ground on the sand.

Out of the darkness
you come, my river,
out of the clouds.
Roads run down to you
and the rivers, Jura and Mitva,
young, from the woods, and loamy
Szeszupe. With poles the loggers
drift by. The ferry
lies on the sand.

And the sky
dark with migrating birds.
In the air of beating wings, high,
reed-sound, well-smoke, smoke of resinous woods.

By the birches above the bank now
the women stand with red
and yellow ribbons – one
draws her daughters
to her swollen belly, the young
sons bathe in the river.

River,
alone always
can I love you
only.
Image of silence.
Plaques for the future: my cry.
Which never held you.
Now in the dark
I hold you fast.

Recall

Fire,
the temptation in the blood:
the comely man. What has passed
is like sleep, dreams
along rivers,
on the waters,
without sail, in the current.

Plains – the lost
villages, the forests' edge.
And a thin smoke
in the air,
straight.

Once,
blubber-lipped, Perkun
came, a feather in his beard,
came in the track of the elk,
the Stutterer came,
travelled the river, drew
darkness, a fishing-net, after him.

There
I was. In the old time.
What is new has never begun. I am a man,
of one flesh with his wife,
who raises his children
for an age without fear.

At the River

Sky,
the blue, old
arch, which goes with
us, which the green
enchants: bank, the lovely
tree, its shadow which
moves on the water.

There is a strip of red,
a trace
of red, we are that red alone
between green and blue,
sky and earth,
when did you say:

'The shadows fly, a
night has called
with owlet voices which came
near under the trees,
the sky was gone'?

Now,
the sky is new,
breath, and no blue,
your temple rests (a slow
beat, no more to be heard,
never more) upon my mouth.

The Death of the Wolf

Between wood and river –
but it is
night, in the moonlight
wolves, the long shadows,
gone. But my boar comes,
stout-hearted, a peasant
eager to reap
his field.

Autumn,
melt away with the
mists! Now a dark season
crouches before the high
wall, before the ice,
the owls swoop over the snow
spitting at dusk,
a sail of sleep,
lost.

But broken. There were
tracks on the road from
the farm. I came with
an axe on my shoulder.
Near the drift
lay the wolf, disembowelled,
its flank savaged.

Pig, I say, brave
little pig, you have put paid
to that devil. I am glad

to hear your snorting,
it makes me warm
in the dark.

Elder-Blossom

Here comes
Babel, Isaak.
He says: In the pogrom
when I was a child
they tore the head
off my pigeon.

Houses in a wooden street,
at the fences, elder.
Down the small steps
the white-scrubbed threshold –
then, you remember,
the flecks of blood.

People, you say: Forget it –
there are young people coming,
their laughter like elder-bushes.
People, the elder
might die
of your forgetfulness.

North Russian Town

(Pustoshka 1941)

Pale
by the road to the North
falls the mountain-wall. The bridge,
the old wood,
the bushy banks.

There the stream lives,
white in the pebbles, blind over the
sand. And the caw of crows
speaks your name: Wind
in the rafters, a smoke
towards the evening.

It comes,
glowing in
the cloud, it follows the winds,
it watches for the fire.

Remote fire breaks forth
in the plain,
far. Who dwell near
forests, on streams, in the wooden
luck of the villages, listen
at evening, lay
an ear to the earth.

Cathedral 1941

Which we saw
across the winter river,
across the black torrent
of the waters, Sophia, sounding
heart of benighted Novgorod.

Once before it was dark.
But a time came,
passing with gay foaming
dolphins, orchards
burnt your cheek, often
behind your fences pilgrims
halted, wet-faced,
in your cupolas' golden cry.

And your night, the moon–abyss,
deathly pale, the halcyon bird
glittered in the icy nest.

Smoke has blackened
your walls, fire broke
your doors, how shall the light
be for your window-sockets.
All was done to our
life, the cry as well
as the silence, we saw
your face, white,
rising over the plains.

Then wrath sprang up
outside
in the marshes.
Wrath, a heavy seed.
How shall I call
one day
my eye still
bright?

Russian Songs

Marina
singing down
from a tower across a landscape
of rocks, three rivers
beneath her feet, but
night and the shadows
of wind in flight.

Beautiful lover,
my tree,
high in your branches
with brow bared
to the moon
I sleep, buried
in my wings.

I sleep —
you give me a grain of salt
scooped from an uncrossed
sea, I give you
a drop of rain
from the land
where no one weeps.

Village

Still the strange land
like drums, distant.
I come down the road.
Under the field-birch
the shepherd, in the rustle of leaves, in the rain-sound
of a cloud. Towards evening
a song of measured tones,
low cries
by the bushes.

Village between marsh and river,
bleak in your early winter's
crow-light – the road around the alders
overgrown, the huts soft with the stain
of rain and peat-smoke – you
my unending light,
my lacklustre light,
written on the edges
of my life, you old light.

Image of the hunter, conjuration,
animal-headed,
painted in the icy
cave, in the rock.

Village Music

Final boat in which I fare
hat no more upon my hair
in four oak-boards smooth and white
rue-sprig in my hand held tight
my friends walk, I ride in state
   someone blows the trumpet
   someone the trombone
boat don't sink beneath my weight
hear the others talking grand:
'this bloke built upon the sand'

From the branchless tree the crow
perched upon the top cries: 'Woe'
from the well-pole tall and trim:
'take the parting gift from him
'take that sprig of rue away
   but there blares the trumpet
   there blares the trombone
no one has removed the spray
all say: 'now he's gone although
'out of time's not far to go

Now I know it and I fare
hat no more upon my hair
moonlight round my beard and brow
too far gone for fooling now
listen as I lie below
   up there sounds the trumpet
   up there the trombone

in the distance calls the crow
I am where I am: in sand
with the rue-sprig in my hand.

Always to be Named

Always to be named:
the tree, the bird in flight,
the reddish rock where the river
flows, green, and the fish
in white smoke, when darkness
falls over the woods.

Signs, colours, it is
a game, I think
it may not end
well.

And who will teach me
what I forgot: the stones'
sleep, the sleep
of the birds in flight, the trees'
sleep, their speech
moves in the darkness – ?

Were there a God
and in the flesh,
and could he call me, I would
walk around, I would
wait a little.

To Klopstock

If I did not want
what is real, this: I say
river and forest,
but I have woven
into my senses the darkness,
voice of the hastening bird, the bowshot
of light round the slope

and the sounding waters –
how would I
speak your name
if a small fame
found me – I have
gathered what I passed,
the shadowed fable of guilt
and atonement:
just as the deeds
I trust – you guided it – I trust
the language of those who forget,
deep into winters
unwinged, I speak its word
of reed.

Language

The tree
greater than the night
with the breath of the valley lakes
with the whisper above
the stillness

The stones
beneath the feet
the shining veins
long in the dust
for ever

Language
worn out
by the weary mouth
on the endless road
to the neighbour's house

The Deserted House

The avenue
defined
by the footsteps of the dead. How the echo
descended over the sea
of air, beneath the trees
ivy creeps, the roots
show, the silence
approaches with birds, white voices.
In the house
walked shadows, a strange conversation
beneath the window. The mice
scurry
through the broken spinet.
I saw an old woman
at the end of the road
in a black shawl
on the stone,
she looked southwards.
Above the sand
with hard split leaves
the thistle bloomed.
There the sky was
opened, in the colour of children's hair.
Earth of beauty fatherland.

Estrangement

Time
walks around
clad
in good luck
and bad luck

Time clad in bad luck
speaks with the clatter
of storks, the storks
avoid him: his plumage
black, his trees shadows,
there is night, his roads
run through the air.

Welebitzy

A jagged patch of red at the end of day
has broken free above the wall of the wood,
a savage light like fires still raging
persists and beside it night is falling.

Stare at the river over the empty fields
until silently sleep numbs your eyes and you
shiver with cold as were it winter
already and all red only a dream.

But then you see the sky and your eyes leap up.
There fires are ablaze and there a forest climbs
so mightily that the earth beneath
seems only a blur and a blind mirror.

TRANSLATORS' NOTE: Welebitzy is a town in Russia.

Urs Oberlin

Flamingo Dance

Come into the evening wind.
It fluffs from the other bank,
Turn light and silver-footed
In the flamingo dance.

Come on cool wings
Into nod, flutter and bow,
The red sun seesaws
Underfoot, and still unuttered,

Cradled in a hundred throats,
The cry with which we greet
The moon when she rises
Rosily from our feathers.

Noon

To encounter a God
is not everyone's thing.
But you don't get asked.
There he stands in the sunken road,
goat-eyed,
the ocean on his horns …
And suddenly
the wind drops.

Who speaks the first
word?

Sand

In Memphis, under the sand,
a house is waiting, your black
sandals are waiting.
The fruit in the garden
has been ripe for a thousand years.
The dead are listening
sandy-lipped: In the honeypot
where the bee drowned
is a buzzing ... still buzzing
... buzzing ...

Ithaca

You
find your way again
down the echo-blue
crag
where the mouth
of silence
drips

there is no-one here
called Eumaeus,
no-one knows you.

Easter Night

Adonis
is risen.
The grass chirps
in the dark valley
and a tremor
wakes distant bells
in the towers:

The sea bore
a head
to the Pythian shore.

The woods
are white with blossom.

Segesta

What do you sacrifice? The lighted altar,
A down-wind into star-surrounded space,
The sudden cool of yew-wreath in your hair,
The parapet, your shadow finds you there
And lifts you to clear silence from the place.

H. C. Artmann

from persian quatrains

2

come stand before my ashen stone
    when the sun sets
recite my pastoral to me
    when the sun sets::
for though the lizard long has gnawed
    my buried heart
yet my verse hovers in the basil still
    when the sun sets

4

just like the candle flame extinguished
    by a gust
will the inscription on my stone
    be lost.
and when as dust my last verse
    falls to dust of earth
soul will like body mix
    as dust with dust

5

a fountain in the night
    that through the window sang::
a rosebush in the night
    that through the window sprang::
a spring moon in the night
    that through the window came:
your flesh. your mouth
    your voice that softly rang

9

expect me at the break of day
    and in the spring:
when from the roses and the dew
    we hear the blackbird sing
then I shall open my cage –
    you will open yours
that freed of bars our hearts
    may each to each take wing

11

within the cup your wine
    is still the morning red
but on your lips
    it turns to evening red:
by God into your hand
    the magic might is given.
that day and night obey you
    in his stead

18

and if your hands should ever
    that young pair
wilt gently like the maple leaf
in the late year –
then as at cockcrow now
    and morning star
I would still say to you:
    come stroke my hair

34

with a white tooth your rose-pale mouth
    bites through the night
as through a blade of sugar.
    never quite
so early has the cock crowed in
    the day –
yet late! cool from the river comes
    the dawn's full flight

37

her huntress' mouth is wet with my
    heart's blood
my heart now trembles in a net
    arrows protrude.
the nightingale has ceased to sing
    in the green depth,
silent the moon climbs from a wound,
    red-shoed

44

a wide and heavy lake, a green land
    fishes know
lies between her and me – even the mountain
    snow
divides us with its strict and
    alpine wall::
come! see! consider her and me
    and go

49

the garden fairy let herself
    be seen
among the roses not upon
    the green:
the grass grows day by day. dawn's
    clearest dew
rises around her. larksong fills
    the scene

54

my steed invades the wood of dream
    again,
tree of dark ivory, where angels
    threaten:
where will the way out be? how will
    this journey end
that brings me nothing the whole night
    but pain?

58

now the swan drifts a pale leaf
    on the pool
with the same pallor the moon pays –
    how cool
to us her light: o night your mouth
    my mouth
so red too red where swan and moon
    hold rule

Heinz Winfried Sabais

Looping Above the West

I

Take-off. And climb. The sun
at your back, Atlas
without an earthly base, escape
into hazard, worthwhile illusion
A few optimistic stanzas
drummed on the copper woods
A fistful of engine-roar
emptied into the aquarium of mankind
The mortar-boards whipped from the heads
of the philosophers of decline – ecstasy!
Slender rocket into the last
deserts of freedom:
Drunk with the spinning horizon
Looping above the West.

2

To be I, without splintering skulls
To be I, without smashing-in ribs
Space! The angry ardour of youth
purged in the tourney of air
in the strutting beat of three motors
through the ogling branch of crows
silver rivers as tinsel
at the edge of deliberate wings
rhythms of almost spiritual lust
arrowed at quivering cirrus and:

To be I, living my own hour –
Dream in the petrol fumes:
Embraced by the horizon
Looping above the West.

3

But startled red signals glow
on the watchful instrument panel
The hour hurtles away
The sun withers
in the yellow potato-field
A dead sky drips
on ramshackle sheds
Below in the bridal bed of hay
a servant-girl conceives
the new epoch, ephemeral lust
My time is blown away
– a little smoke in the wind:
Imprisoned by the horizon
Looping above the West.

Generation

for Krolow

I

Jeunesse d'acier, international,
exchanging pass-words with no-one.
All the watch-fires are out, the
last logs covered with frost.
Our best cogitations dwell
in the rotted shin-bone that a peasant,
far away on the Dnieper,
far away on the Elbe,
tosses from his field, verses with
earth between the teeth,
decline without a bronze
autumn, downfall buried
by time, meaning
made obsolete by history,
no logic, no consolation,
mathematics too is no longer
valid: One was
not one but your life.
And for those who daub
him in ash upon our
foreheads, god is made ashamed.

2

Let silence rest upon
us. We read off
the text (like lovers)
from the pulsing morse
of the carotid artery
and recognize every intention
(like boxers under attack)
by the expression of the iris.
Our concepts are
sensitive and empirical.
Say: Flowery mead and we
think of fox-hole and
entrenching tools. Say:
Man – with Schiller and
Pascal – and we associate
exactly: stomach-wound, execution,
political police and all the
cunnings of self-preservation.
We do not use the words
'Passed away' when we write of
death. Our metaphors are
loaded with phosphorus.
They burn.

3

All done with? Who knows?
The hands of the clock move
around a mechanical axis,
but time strikes its hours
on our diaphragm. – Making
money, that can be
arranged, the finished product and
the brief to counsel as ordered, and
the thirty manual operations
for landing a bomber
still exactly in mind. At evening
sausages on sticks and several
cocktails, and the car waiting
outside for the carnival
of feeling to end.
Now and then the 'warmth of the nest'.
But never quite thawed out.
Steel filings in the blood and
at night the trails of nomads
crossing the brain, to the
moon? to Mars? Ah, only
a crippled gaze
follows them. And Venus
comforts with an anxiously
ready womb.

4

Jeunesse d'acier, slowly
eaten by rust, Roland,
whom they omitted to kill,
now in retirement. At twenty
led attacks, commanded
U-boats, aimed bombs.
At thirty veterans, collecting
administrative experience, and
studying the laws of natural
corruption almost with
indifference. No blow
is so strong that it shakes
the centre where the unrecountable
dream dwells – which doesn't
help. Sometimes in a
frivolous mood or
in re-won folly
we forget those two who
rot for the third.
But otherwise optimism remains
a symptom of old age, too
early for us, too childish.
The white blocks of new
bazaars, nickel and chrome,
are only a seduction
of the retina, progress is
pulped newspaper, the chambers
of the heart are leaded and
the dust of already re-utilized
debris will lie long
on our lids.

5

But: Beauty, Love, Courage?
No, only the torment of traumatic
revisions which are without
significance in philosophy!
That was Beauty: a
sunrise. We parachuted
down on the bridgehead. The
machineguns pointed upward. Sunrise.
And Love: Pale faces
which one strove to face in silence
or a willing body and
thirty minutes. Luck too:
amputation was not necessary.
Art: when one banked
steeply enough to get out of
the line of fire. Honour:
exchanged for bread while a
prisoner-of-war or deleted for the sake
of strange outrages. Courage:
sold as a job lot during third degree.
The Inner Life: very decimated
and disowned; for the old shamans,
specialists in the psyche, mix new
and effective poisons. But: Peace?
Frieden? *Pace*? – the weapons
are brought up to date.
And Truth is: the lie
which we love.

6

Jeunesse d'acier, generation
without youth, without age, a
cracked bell in the head,
discord in the pleasant peal
of antique ideas. No specimen.
Wordless drama. Had they
nothing to till? – Graveyards!
And the historical achievement?
So-and-so many million fallen.
What that is, is known here and there –
to an old woman who has
no more tears, to a pensioner
who studies the atlas because
a strange place-name will
not come to mind, to a child
who is shown a yellowing
photograph: That was
your father. Later, perhaps,
a dilettante, questioning history,
will find: Their wordlessness was
an Odyssey, two thousand years
after Christ, when concentration camps,
boycott and the hydrogen bomb
were invented. The rest
is silence.

Shall We Meet Again

Shall we meet again
in the wordless wastes beyond us
where caravans of the dead are travelling
uncertainly towards the Oasis
Nowhere or God?

Shall I still know your name
when the body's memory
flakes cruelly away and your image
is extinguished as my
last thoughts break apart?

Shall I still keep your love
where the edge of the great shadow
strikes me and numbs the sweet unrest
What will remain once eternity's
hate melts the foolish flesh?

Who will lend us eyes for each other
in the laconic solemnity of nothing
when the wave of earthly time freezes
glassy before our feet
and no desire moves it?

Shall we meet again
in the wordless wastes beyond us
in the swaying shadows of uncertain caravans
in the Oasis Nowhere or God
deep in untimely snow?

Socialist Elegy

... and there would be nothing left
to us but to bewail our state of slavery.
SOLZHENITSYN

I

We, born in back-street slums,
in the days of the proletariat;
narrowness, constraint, a stable warmth without
share capital, interest-free,
human material meant
for immediate consumption: learning
in order to be of use; culture
amuses the gentry. Trained
from first youth for the mass grave. Nevertheless,
despite knee bends, despite humiliations,
self-determination from within,
cajoled pleasure, my
cajoled life, be as
it may, my life!
Let a thousand flowers, a thousand
obscene curses blossom above the
murderous collectivisms
of this wretched century!
Fascism, communism and
so on forever, *merde*, no thanks!
The parliamentary foot in the door
to all power and, nicely calculated,
social legislation in the till!
And the Rights of Man

nowhere lost sight of
for a moment.
The dignity of man,
mine, yours, his, hers,
ours, yours, theirs, always
taken concretely and
given too, outmoded measure
of that not to be relinquished:
better to die than crawl.

2

That would have been that then:
Marching orders straight
across Europe. To kill
or be killed.
Hunched solidarity
with those who suffered.
Melancholy amid bloody vomit
and lies and hate.
Montaigne in the knapsack,
that endured. Educated
by retreats, fleeing
from victory to victory. The
lesson of our lives:
The senseless
machinery of might,
greased with degenerate
ideals. Optimism was
betrayal of your neighbour. The cleverest
technique of survival:
To abandon everything, let go,

lose, in order to keep
yourself. Moments
alone, with two or three gathered
together, never more. The sum total:
Systemized happiness is organized
misery, the unspoiled world
a crematorium-dream.
Nothing is worth it, nothing, nothing at all,
to kill, to let yourself be killed.
This as experience.

3

That would have been that then:
Surviving with effort
both the Brown and Red
benefactors of mankind. Clearing
rubble, starving,
begging. Marriage, work,
discovering duties, coddling
the offspring, writing
books for no one, helping
to built new cities, practice.
Reason too – holding high
the gay and free in muck
and luck. No line, certainly, only
the erratic succession of very
individual points in approximation.
But history is not designed for you
nor for a single generation.
You have only your
lifetime, one lifetime, and

you realize that very slowly.
Little enough, acquired:
books, pictures, enough to live on
for a year and too much
moral surplus,
not to be consumed by moods.
An unconcern with real estate –
never be static. One
must be able to withdraw,
now, always. Off into the
woods, grey-head, get away
when the lemmings come.
To be free as a bird,
prepared in the end
to be an outlaw, the one thing
that costs nothing, at most
your head.

4

The generation that is, that will have been:
the bled-white generation,
squashed, historically, between
tyrannical fathers
('Gott mit uns!')
and fanaticized grandsons
(Marx mit uns!)
theory-gorged frenzy,
which wants simple totality
instead of difficult truth,
madly rebreeds its own stupidity –
to the nuclear *éclat!*

We are still here, cool as autumn,
the sceptical coolies,
shall soon be gone.
And now abideth:
Fugitive trace elements
of humanity in this
and that for a while;
soon a manipulated saga,
a counterfeit smile
in the social concrete, finally
wastepaper, nothing, nothing at all.

5

Poke fun at yourselves,
Epigoni, sheep in wolves' clothing,
on your noisy march
from concentration camp to concentration camp.
Know-it-alls, know-nothings!
In all perfect systems –
believed, thought-out –
inquisition breeds.
Your closed image of the world,
a penitentiary: a relapse into
'self-induced infancy'.
Many doors are open to fools,
no exit; there are only
escape routes over the wall.
Stalin in Marx,
like the doll inside the doll.
Do you want to dance
again the bestial dance

of death? Why? What for?
Another GULAG society?
Long live Eduard Bernstein
and the strict Socialist Commonwealth!
That requires work,
however, not opium.
Sweat out, lemmings, what
you have learned by heart,
the intoxicating illusion!
Your Mayakovskys praise
murder – with suicide
already in their skulls.
Your revolution will
devour you (big eats!)
like hot fish-fingers.
The frost of your fire, you can do it,
will glaciate Europe, or
with luck (furtively)
you will escape yourselves.

6

May our dust in that day
lie light upon you,
a useful hacking cough
for your computers. And
an ancient nuisance
to your Chinese bosses.

1974

from *Self or Saxifrage*

3

The cherry trees lining the road to Leuthen
stood on land my grandfather leased. We stayed
there in a hut in summer with our dogs
scaring away the starlings and picking cherries.
To the south loomed Zobten, the sacred hill,
where herds of cloud grazed slowly towards the east.
Potatoes grew over the soldiers' graves.
A cool breeze came from the woods near the Oder.
In the old chestnut tree on the hill
I sat and sang and the birds listened.

9

I received my baptism of fire in the ancient manner
at my father's side in a streetfight
between the Browns and Reds. We lay in the entrance
to a coal-cellar opposite their headquarters pub.
Windows shattered above our heads, they were shooting.
Hand-grenades now, said my father (Third Regiment
    of Footguards).
The police reassembled the republic.
Legality, yes, there ought to be legality. Law for all.
But soon force was stronger, our spirits sank.
Did not want to sacrifice ourselves and were sacrificed.

19

The synagogue burns. Its Menetekel
inscribes the brows of the startled multitude.
Who will preserve your house if the house of God is
    burning?
What are you worth if certain other men,
placard around the neck, are maltreated?
If they are robbed and murdered by the state today
you could be robbed and murdered by the state tomorrow.
November thirty-eight. And I hear my father
whisper from behind his newspaper:
From now on, son, it's every man for himself.

27

The red cracked lips
of my beloved, my wife, and
the touching bundle beside her
with eyes, nose, mouth – our child.
My senses were still blunt
with the noise of battle,
sweat of fear, smell of death;
then came that light,
a tiny star in the midst
of barbarism, alpha and omega.

44

As they laid upon me
the gold chain of office and I
saw the resignation in my
predecessor's eyes, I felt
the chill of history:
Expect no gratitude and be thankful
when you reap no ingratitude –
I am not too bad
to fail, not too good
to be of use, I said.

59

He looked almost worried
and suddenly pulled my ear:
'Do you have to die now?'
'Perhaps, who knows' I
replied. 'No' insisted my grandson,
that little bundle of energy
that couldn't yet read or write,
'I want you to tell me
a story!' 'Which
story?' 'Hans in Luck!'

90

We circle pointlessly, aimlessly, endlessly, Amen.
Imagination may talk a great deal:
He wanted to, ought to have, had, was;
that too will soon sleep in the dark:
Saxifrage on solid magma,
sheet lightning in night and ice.
New fates are jumbled in the shaken bag.
Atoms dance, possibilities swirl,
nothing can be foretold. And your
mystery remains impenetrable: *Lumen mundi.*

1981

Wolfgang Bächler

Autumn in Vaucluse

The last peasant
shuts his barn,
saddles his mule
and rides down the sky.
His shadow glides over the earth.

A black tangle
of cats
romps on the cemetery-wall.
Fingers of the dead,
cypresses,
point into the enormous
stretch of net,
the web of rays
spun by the light.

A squadron of birds,
whipped south by the wind-god
from the Autumn paradise of the Ile-de-France,
thrusts in vain against the mesh.
With threads of light in the feathers
and waves of light in the throat
they fall back to earth exhausted.
You too are trapped.

The grapes drip blue
down the vineyard
on the pale dry
skeleton of the river.
The lines and planes

of burnt ochre
always show you the same
law of geometry

Thyme shoots
from fissure and window
of deserted farms,
undergrowth blazes.
Swathes of myrtle-leaf billow
through rotting branches
of denuded roof-beams.

Even the sleeping bats still hear
the staccato cadence of the cicada:
    You too are trapped.
The grapes drip red
    down the vineyard.

Rachel

'Gardez cet objet précieusement!'
said Vincent van Gogh to Rachel
to whom he gave his ear.
I looked in vain for that 'Maison de la tolérance'
number one rue du Bout-d'Arles,
where according to the chronicle this occurred.

I encountered Rachel at noon.
Beneath the black cypresses
of Aliscamp, the Elysian fields,
she sat on a broken lid
of a Roman sarcophagus.
Beetles crawled from between her toes
up her naked thighs.

A huge ear, spotlessly white,
with deep, darkening convolutions
lay in her lap.
Through the lowered claws of her lashes
her eyes glowed so strongly
that the agave in front of her began to burn.

Then I saw the well.
I rolled the stone from the shaft:
Laban's sheep came to drink.
Wide and open against the sky
is the house of tolerance,
immortal Rachel,
who does not want to be comforted.

Burial

near Apt in Provence

A peasant tied his rabid dog
to the trunk of an olive-tree.
Mad with rage the slavering beast
bit its pain into the bark.

The peasant's shot
cut the drumskin
of the cicada,
tore the net
of the spider of the light,
hacked a hole in the sky.
The smoke hung black
in the olive-branches.

The peasant's mattock
cut the coarse coat of turf,
tore the net of the tangled root,
hacked a hole in the earth.
The dust hung red
in the olive-branches.

The peasant untied
the leash from the trunk,
the dog from the leash,
shoved it into the hole,
threw three handfuls of earth
on the yellow-brown-spotted
purple-flecked hide,

shovelled the cut sods,
the torn roots,
the hacked clods over it
and stamped the earth flat.

Cicada drum
the hide vibrates
the sun spins light.
The skin of the sky
is a scarless blue,
the scar in the grass
caput-mortuum-red.
A flying hound hangs
in the olive-branches.

Deserted Paradise

Ile-de-France

Ruined walls over which the green
foams out into the fallow fields.
At the entrance a dead adder.
A pigeon's-wing hangs in the thornbush.
Stinging nettles, twigs and brambles
enclose the lizard's kingdom,
protect the birds' breeding-ground.

    In Celtic times
    the priests cut
    the mistletoe
    from the tree
    with golden sickles.

The mistletoe still flourishes
on these ancient trees,
stronger, more lovely than ever.
But now no-one knows
its magic, its powers of healing.
No priest, no gardener
prunes the boughs.
Only ivy climbs up
to the mistletoe.
The two have vanquished the oaks.

The petrified gods
mourn by the wayside,
blackened by rain,
clothed to the breast in fern.

Betrayed and deserted by men,
they too have lost their innocence,
widowed, orphaned,
forgotten the joy of their nakedness.

The wind throws
down to them
apples and nuts.
They do not take them.
They eat their own shadow
at noon
and drink the light at evening.

The seeds in the apple wither.
The chestnut bursts
its own shell.
The shining skin
wrinkles in the grass.
In the nutshells
mummified priests
shrink towards resurrection.

But no man comes
to crack the nuts,
no woman returns
to gather the apples,
no child to collect the chestnuts.
The nettles sting themselves.

Blackberry-blood drips
on the pigeons feathers.
The birds cry in the thornbush.
Flies assemble

on the body of the snake.
The lizards snap at the flies.
Snails glide in
to conquer their kingdom.

Elisabeth Borchers

Now It Sings – Now It Laments

I

Now it sings:
sings lovely and lively
in the clouds
which wash the sky blue
and the sky falls falls
into lakes, country-schools and clothes

Now it sings:
harlequin on the bridge
spits into the boats
which are white
on the captains
who are blue
and fishes for waves
letting the fish live
hi there, tell me something of love

Now it sings:
I am the poppy
drowsing
and am the key to the heart
enter be verily fed and sweet

Now it sings:
we are the days of the berries
build us a nest
in which the swallows can bathe

Thus it sings
and on the typewriters
the poets lay their heads
when their voices die away
in the great singing

2

Now it laments:
do you always come so late
peeled off the mouths of ivory
cracked melted
silver fish-work
stands frozen in the lake
across the walls
the wind hunts
with naked knives

Now it laments:
do you always come so late
always between two summers
always when up and down
the mice begin
to run faster
you always come so late
when all is already asleep
when nothing is softer
than sleep
when only your voice
swirls from heaven
with the snow
and begins to sing

To Someone In Hiding

I don't want
you to hide
the loud shall be loud
and the soft be soft

I know no one
who stands upright
when he bends his back
or wears a coat well
which is too tight

Show yourself
only the wind
walks up and down the streets

The day after tomorrow
I shall fetch you

The Song

The minstrel plays
a child repeats the song

A song that goes
but how does it go
the man in the moon
he sits in the moon
they are singing for their lives

Who doesn't come now
will come too late
the two are already going away

There Was a Summer Once

We have hung around long enough
now the sun
faints
it stings no more

The trees end
the wave hangs so heavy
how ordinary things have become
how ordinary

I laid a bet
that the summer would stay

Progress

Every day
the world grows smaller
by the breadth of a cornfield

Many have only
half a bed

There are dogs in the front yard
tearing
their master to pieces

Christa Reinig

The Tightrope Walker

When you drop slowly from a lower rung
and sink into the sand as if you fell
you feel how shakily the earth is strung
no footing here is kept by skill

I work on principle without a net
and never think about the height at all
a step a spring – for each the rule is set
I can't imagine how to fall

then peering through binoculars which show
tower-deep before your face a spider's thread
you crunch a bit of peppermint and know
that the last time it won't succeed

The Hangman

With collar open at the throat
he takes his place on the trap-door
and downs the tot his warder brought
because he wished for nothing more

the apprentice slips the rope about
his master's neck with much display
ties all his care into the knot –
at most he hears the hangman say:

now do the job as good as me
see that the knot sits as it ought
before you step back finally
and show what you've been taught

The Three Questioners

I ask the blokes who did the kicking
I threw myself down in the road:
yes I betrayed him I was shrieking
I ask you boys, who never did

that day we burned beneath the breastplate
our blood ran cold at every blow
it's no use keeping on about it
nor asking what you'll never know

I never played dice with you neither
you're lying, where's the dice we tossed
we gambled for his coat together
the dice were loaded, and I lost

Cats' Constitution

Proud-tailed romans
let us be dull of understanding
forepawish tolerant
obstinately haunched
bearers of the order of the
disdainful whisker

allegro
menuetto mastless
adagio cantabile
presto

elephants blow tin trumpets
stallions prance
in step
St Bernards carry brandy-casks
we don't

The Ballad of Bloody Bomme

Most distinguished audience
don't get tough or take offence
if our tale should sound absurd
the absurdest ever heard
are the tales the dear lord tells
no emotion in me wells
when I come to draw a breath
and speak of my friend Bomme's death

may you never meet the fate
which our pictures illustrate

In court the bloodstained tie is shown
as exhibit number one
of the loot though not a trace
those who cannot find a place
stand outside and hear the noise
for the prisoner enjoys
making fools of judge and jury
and the public laughs like fury

it's obvious that no one digs
the chaps who sit there wearing wigs

Iron door and iron bed
with the closet near its head
pleased as punch the warder grows
to meet again a man he knows
resting now no more to roam
Bomme feels himself at home
a rich man too finds coffined rest
holds the lid down to his chest

with this man now wealth and all
Bomme's not concerned at all

The warder says: now listen mate
take it easy – get this straight
since you've got to lose your head
you won't be too badly fed
you play ball with me and I
will watch you with my wooden eye
Bomme tense already scrawls
little men upon the walls

crossing fingers won't help here
Bomme's head must disappear

Bomme sees no urgency
for last rites and eternity
when the parson comes to tell
how a man condemned to hell
suffers torment till he cries
turns and tosses – Bomme sighs:
that is interesting I'm sure
but I've heard it all before

how can a true christian know
what the man is feeling now

Bomme in the prison yard
never working very hard
helps to build the guillotine
finally the dread machine
towers above him high and holy
Bomme looks and murmurs: golly
this is worse than fascism
and tries out the mechanism

what justice is he comprehends
as the heavy blade descends

Getting up before the fowls
that hits Bomme in the bowels
rubbing freezing hands our friend
concentrates upon the end
doesn't really want to pray
with the bog so far away
then he thinks: oh what the hell
I'll get over this as well

realises in other words
that one stone will kill both birds

If his mother were not dead
tears in torrents would be shed
no such feelings now distract
from the cold official act
Bomme is struck off the books
And put in a wooden box
a convict sighs – because they say
he's got to wash the blood away

will you all forgive us please
a tale of such indecencies

but all who liked the sound of that
can put a penny in the hat

Günter Bruno Fuchs

The Raven

The raven sleeping in the shade
sings silently and dreams of lantern-light
and gathers silence in and flies towards the night

raising the top-hat from his head
to lighted lamps and headstones white
and to himself there, sleeping in the shade.

Demurrer

Take it easy, didn't
want to do
nuffink
to that lad of
eleven. Only wanted
to take 'im
into the lav, only
wanted
to show 'im
what sort of blokes
there are about. That they
chat up
lads of his age
and want to
take 'em
into the lav
as if
there was nuffink
at all
in doing that.

Prison Window

As little
kids
they was
so chuffed
with the
sun that they
chalked

the sun

up
everywhere, how

you forgets
little
fings
like that.

Preservation of Monuments

The man says
Cockledoodledo. The man
says Wotcher. The man
says: Christ, the
ruin ain't
a bloody lav!

That's what
the man
said
as he went by
that's what
he said. And

he was
right: the
ruin ain't
a bloody
lav.

Homework

Progress
couldn't care bleedin' less
about me. And
as far as I'm concerned, I
couldn't care bleedin' less
about

Progress. Cos
we was
there first
wasn't we,
as 'umans.

So put
that down
in your notebook
my lad.

For a Child

I have prayed. Take a share of the sun and go.
The trees will be in leaf.
I have told the blossoms to adorn you.

When you come to the river a ferryman will be waiting.
At night his heart sounds across the water.
His boat has golden timbers, it will carry you.

The shores will be inhabited.
I have told those who dwell there to love you.
You will be met by someone who has heard me.

Christian Geissler

house in friesland dying-in home
sterile in low-flying fighter terrain
of F104s from wittmund

in corridor-trenches
between white sheets
feeling the sharp edge of death

the cry of the fish in the corner tank
reverberating shadowless
beneath lights that never go out

'AT NOON ...'

at noon
when the dinner bells ring
I offer my mother my arm
leading her over the manmade carpet
I walk at her side
over plastic mosaic
soon we shall breathe the swelling scent
of porkbelly and sprayed disinfectant
when at last we reach the gate of saucepans
I let her go on ahead
into draggle and clatter
my mother
raises her arm
to them all
shouting through the glass of the fake state coach
throwing tiny things down from rigging-loft railings
wordlessly
pope elisabeth

noone here lines the streets
noone bends the knee in exultation

alone porkbelly potatoes and beans
alone my mother
not inconsolable

'LOOK ...'

look

says my mother
the heavy stones
in the garden

under them grass and leaves
tried
to grow in the dark

look my yellow hand

look

says my mother
hardly a man here
they die first
the price of power

one was a captain
river shipping
lost all three sons in the war
highly respected

now he's sick
we know he's going
sometimes I look
then I think where

but then he says to me
stopping then
silent with silence
having to blubber tears

feel ashamed be afraid ask
stealing a look at the door
if it is possible
admissible expected offensive forbidden

if he asked me
to stroke his arm
to stroke the inside
of his arm

look my cold hand

'EVENINGS ...'

evenings
the motionless corridors
broad square narrowing at the end
a void of striplighting above

at my back
at my heels
my mother's door
not yet closed

watching me go
watching
wanting to wave
I do not look round

at all these doors
trapdoors
black in the crack
nothing but mothers

an eye searching whispers a pricked-up ear
between fire extinguishers and veiltail
on wipeable rubber sheets
near the exit-doors

for there is the way out
for there must still be something still to come
mostly mute
the final nights of the mothers

Horst Bienek

katorga   Russian for 'forced labour'

Vorkuta

In Vorkuta no disciple of the Lord
walks the green-foaming tundra,
Here there is no feeding of the five thousand.
Here a dream dies every day
In the still uncertain dawn.

In Vorkuta, no machine-guns rust.
Whoever tires listens to the cantata
of the snowstorm in the barbed wire
and embroiders with his own blood
an endless pattern in his black katorga-shirt.

Nor in Vorkuta
is the prayer of the dead a prayer
and the lips of the living
are rusting lips, iron bars,
behind which the tongue festers and rots.

In Vorkuta no widow
covers her hair with a veil.
Her breasts still tremble
when she thinks of the loneliness
beneath the arching body of a man.

In Vorkuta no one digs a grave
for crumbling hopes
And there is no one to weep
when the abandoned corpses
drift to the rivers with the melting snow.

Vorkuta, 1953

Dream-Galley

The moon is taut above the stream
Where sleeplessly the fishes spawn.
The starry winds are banished now,
The morse of day is heard at dawn.

In gaol you see the sun's first rays
Caught where the rifle-barrels gleam:
And through that curtain of blue steel
You must escape. The ship of dream

Conveys you to the edge of light.
And then the shooting in the yard.
The hot lead that you scarcely feel,
The rivers, echoing, unheard.

The Myth of Time

The myth of time disintegrates
The birds mourn softly in the wind
You chose the cell in which you sleep
That truth might live you passed the gates
And wedded to the dream you weep
The birds mourn softly in the wind
The myth of time disintegrates

The Alphabet

for Nelly Sachs

Where pain is
       there is room for nothing else
Pain is everything:
       there are no hands to the clock
       no coins
       no weapons
       no prayers
             Wind and tree exist no more
            no colours no pictures
       no more formulas
       no more coordinates
       no hiding-places
       no quotations
       no enemies

There is only one alphabet left:
       pain

Assembly

The eye of the butcher in the crowd –

       He divides
       those to be slaughtered
       from those fit for breeding
       with a practised glance
and classifies them casually
       according to weight age and quality
his only
       wish is
          to see them hanging
             in their rosy flesh
head down
          quartered
the purple mark of the god
          on their ear-lobes

       As his murderer's eye falls upon me
       I feel his contempt
       his knife remains unopened
       He consigns me to the knacker's yard

H. C. Artmann

H. C. ARTMANN (Hans Carl) was born in Achatz am Walde, Austria in 1921. He was a poet, playwright, novelist and translator who first became widely known for his dialect poems. He lived in Vienna where, in the fifties, he was a leading member of the 'Wiener Gruppe'. Later he lived in Stockholm. He died in 2000.

Wolfgang Bächler

WOLFGANG BÄCHLER was born in Augsburg in 1925. He was the youngest co-founder of the 'Gruppe 47' which has played an important role in postwar German literature. Bächler began to write poems in 1943 and published his first book in 1950. He became a literary and theatre critic. In 1956 he moved to France where he lived for many years. He died in Munich in 2007.

Horst Bienek

HORST BIENEK was born in 1930 in Gleiwitz, Upper Silesia. He died in 1990. He began his literary career as a journalist in Berlin, while studying with Brecht at the Berliner Ensemble. In 1951 he was arrested in East Berlin on a political charge and sentenced to twenty-five years' forced labour, of which he served four years in the prison camp of Varkuta, in Russia. He was freed by an amnesty in 1955 and afterwards lived in West Germany. Among his prose works was the prize-winning novel *The Cell*.

Johannes Bobrowski

JOHANNES BOBROWSKI was born in Tilsit in East Prussia in 1917. He spent part of his boyhood on his grandfather's farm in Lithuania. He was educated in Rastenburg and Königsberg and was studying art history in Berlin when he was conscripted in 1939. He took part in the military campaigns in Poland, France and Russia. He was a prisoner-of-war in Russia until 1949. After his release he worked as a publisher's editor in East Berlin. He wrote poetry, novels and short stories. His poems were first published in *Das Innere Reich*, the Nazi cultural periodical, in 1943. His poems next appeared in the East Berlin Communist magazine *Sinn und Form* ten years later. He died in 1965.

Elisabeth Borchers

ELISABETH BORCHERS was born in 1926 in Homberg on the Rhine. She grew up in Alsace. She has lived for periods in France and the USA. Her first volume of poetry appeared in 1961. She has made translations from the French and is the author of a collection of radio plays the title work of which was awarded an important prize by South German Radio. She has worked as an editor in publishing houses.

Günter Bruno Fuchs

GÜNTER BRUNO FUCHS was born in Berlin in 1928 and died in East Berlin in 1977. At the age of 14 he was called into the anti-aircraft searchlight service and then into the Labour Service. Later he was in action at the front. He was taken prisoner of war by the Belgians and released when he was 17. After the war he worked at many different jobs, from building worker to circus clown. He studied at the Berlin Academy for Art. In 1958 he was co-founder of the Berlin Gallery 'zinke'. Fuchs was a member of the New Friedrichshagen Poets' Circle of which Johannes Bobrowski was the last president.

Christian Geissler

CHRISTIAN GEISSLER was born in Hamburg in 1928. He has worked as a freelance in radio and television dramatic and documentary programmes. He has been a member of the editorial staff of two magazines and written several novels. From 1972 to 1974 he taught at the German Film and Television Academy in West Berlin. He lives in Hamburg.

Max Hölzer

MAX HÖLZER (1915–1984) was born in Graz in Austria. He was for many years a lawyer. He edited *Surrealistiche Publicationen*, 1950–2, the first post-1945 magazine to publish French Surrealistic writers. He lived for a number of years in Paris. He translated Sarraute, Breton, Bataille, Constant and Rousseau into German.

Urs Oberlin

URS OBERLIN was born in Bern, Switzerland in 1919. He studied law and dental medicine in Fribourg and Bern and obtained his doctorate in Düsseldorf. He lived for long periods in Sicily and Calabria. He has travelled widely in the Far East, India, Ceylon, Africa, Greece and Europe. He lives in Zurich. In addition he has published novels and is co-author of an archaeological study. He translates Italian and French poetry. He died in June 2008.

Christa Reinig

CHRISTA REINIG was born in 1926 in Berlin where, after leaving school, she worked in a number of different jobs ranging from florist to factory worker. From 1950 to 1953 she studied at the Workers and Peasants College, Berlin and until 1957 she studied the history of art and archaeology at the Humbolt University in Berlin. From 1957 to 1963 she was a scientific assistant at the Märkische Museum in East Berlin. In 1964 she was awarded the Bremen Literature Prize. After the ceremony she remained in West Germany.

Heinz Winfried Sabais

HEINZ WINFRIED SABAIS was born in 1922 in Breslau. He studied literature and philosophy at the University of Jena. During the War he was a pilot in the German air force. After the war he worked as a publisher's editor and civil servant in East Germany. In 1950 he fled to West Germany where he was accorded the status of a political refugee, 'with life and limb in danger'. After working as a journalist for a time in West Berlin he moved to Darmstadt where he filled several cultural positions. He was elected to the city council in 1963 and in 1971 elected Chief Burgomaster of Darmstadt. He died in 1981.

Nelly Sachs

NELLY SACHS was born in Berlin in 1891. Although she wrote and published verse from the age of seventeen she remained virtually unrecognised. When the Nazis came to power she lived in isolation, taking refuge in the works of the German and Jewish mystics who greatly influenced her poetry. In 1940, accompanied by her sixty-nine year old mother, she escaped to Sweden. She lived in Stockholm and continued to write in German. In 1966 she received the Nobel Prize for Literature. She died in 1970.

ACKNOWLEDGEMENTS

H. C. Artmann

Text: *American German Review*, Vol. XXXVI No. 3, 1970.

The original poems are from *persische qvatrainen*, collispress, Hommerich, 1966. By kind permission of Suhrkamp Verlag GmbH & Co. KG. All rights reserved.

Wolfgang Bächler

Text: *Doors of Smoke*, Satis, 1991.

These poems are taken from *Türen aus Rauch* © 1963 Insel Verlag, Frankfurt am Main. By kind permission of Suhrkamp Verlag GmbH & Co. KG. All rights reserved.

Horst Bienek

Text: *Horst Bienek* in Unicorn German Series, Unicorn Press, Santa Barbara, 1969. *Johannes Bobrowski and Horst Bienek: Selected Poems*, Penguin Modern European Poets, Penguin Books, 1971.

The poems by Horst Bienek were published in *Traumbuch eines Gefangenen*, copyright © Carl Hanser Verlag, Munich, 1957, and *was war was ist*, copyright © Carl Hanser Verlag, Munich, 1966. Grateful acknowledgement is made to the publishers.

Johannes Bobrowski

Text: *Shadow Lands*, Anvil, 1984; 'Welebitzy', first printed in *Das Innere Reich*, March 1944, from *Agenda* Vol. 32 No 2, 1994.

The poems are from *Sarmatische Zeit*, © Deutsche Verlags-Anstalt 1961; *Schattenland Ströme*, © Deutsche Verlags-Anstalt 1962 and *Wetterzeichen*, © Union Verlag 1966. 'Pruzzian Elegy' appeared in the Union Verlag edition of *Sarmatische Zeit*, 1961. We thank Deutsche Verlags-Anstalt, Munich, a member of Verlagsgruppe Random House GmbH, for permission to use these poems which are collected in *Gesammelte Werke in sechs Bänden*, Band 1, © 1988.

ELISABETH BORCHERS

Text: *Elisabeth Borchers*, Unicorn German Series, Unicorn Press, Santa Barbara, 1969.

Selected from *Gedichte* © Herman Luchterhand Verlag GmbH, Neuwied and Berlin, 1961, and *Der Tisch an dem wir sitzen* © Herman Luchterhand Verlag GmbH, Neuwied and Berlin, 1967. By kind permission of Suhrkamp Verlag GmbH & Co. KG. All rights reserved.

GÜNTER BRUNO FUCHS

Text: *The Raven*, Satis, 1984.

These poems are taken from *Das Lesebuch des Günter Bruno Fuchs* © Carl Hanser Verlag, Munich 1970. Grateful acknowledgement is made to the publishers.

CHRISTIAN GEISSLER

Text: *Songs from the Old Folk's Home*, Satis, 1988.

These poems are taken from *Im Vorfeld einer Schussverletzung* © Rotbuch Verlag Berlin 1980. Grateful acknowledgement is made to the publishers.

MAX HÖLZER

Text: *Amfortiade*, Satis, 1968; *German Writing Today* ed. by Christopher Middleton, Penguin Books, 1967.

The poems are from *Nigredo* by Max Hölzer © Insel Verlag Frankfurt am Main 1962. By kind permission of Suhrkamp Verlag GmbH & Co. KG. All rights reserved.

URS OBERLIN

Text: *Flamingo Dance*, Satis, 1991.

These poems are taken from *Gedichte* (Claassen, 1961). Grateful acknowledgment is made to Bonnier Media Deutschland GmbH.

CHRISTA REINIG

Text: *The Tightrope Walker*, Satis, 1981.

These poems are taken from *Steine von Finisterre* by Christa Reinig, copyright © Verlag Eremiten-Presse, Düsseldorf, 1960, 1974. Grateful acknowledgement is made to the author and publishers.

HEINZ WINFRIED SABAIS

Text: *The People and the Stones*, Anvil, 1983.

Grateful acknowledgement is made to Frau Ingeborg Sabais for permission to reprint the poems whose originals appeared in *Looping über dem Abendland*, Georg Büchner Verlag, 1956; *Mitteilungen/Communications*, © Eduard Roether Verlag 1971; *Sozialistische Elegie*, © Eduard Roether Verlag 1975 and *Selbst oder Saxifraga*, © J.G. Blüschke Verlag 1981.

NELLY SACHS

Text (with other translators): *O The Chimneys*, Farrar, Straus and Giroux Inc., New York, 1967; *Nelly Sachs: Selected Poems*, copyright © 1967 by Farrar, Straus and Giroux Inc., New York, first published in Great Britain by Jonathan Cape, 1968; *The Seeker*, Farrar, Straus and Giroux Inc., New York, 1970. These translations appear in *Abba Kovner and Nelly Sachs: Selected Poems*, Penguin Modern European Poets, Penguin Books, 1971.

The poems by Nelly Sachs are taken from *Fahrt im Staublose*, copyright © Suhrkamp Verlag, Frankfurt am Main, 1962; *Späte Gedichte*, copyright © Suhrkamp Verlag, Frankfurt am Main, 1965. By kind permission of Suhrkamp Verlag GmbH & Co. KG. All rights reserved.

Some modern German poetry from Anvil

Johannes Bobrowski
Shadow Lands
SELECTED POEMS
Translated by Ruth and Matthew Mead

Elisabeth Borchers
Fish Magic
SELECTED POEMS
Translated by Anneliese Wagner

Paul Celan
Poems of Paul Celan
Translated and introduced by Michael Hamburger

Sarah Kirsch
Winter Music
SELECTED POEMS
Translated by Margitt Lehbert

Rainer Maria Rilke
Turning-Point
MISCELLANEOUS POEMS 1912–1926
Translated by Michael Hamburger

Heinz Winfried Sabais
The People and the Stones
SELECTED POEMS
Translated by Ruth and Matthew Mead

Georg Trakl
The Poems of Georg Trakl
Translated by Margitt Lehbert

Some classic German poetry from Anvil

TRANSLATED BY MICHAEL HAMBURGER

Goethe: *Roman Elegies*
and other poems

Johann Wolfgang von Goethe (1749–1832) is mainly known in the English-speaking world as the poet of *Faust*. His other poetry, for all its richness and variety, has received comparatively little attention. This edition collects all the versions made over many years by Michael Hamburger. His selection and introduction provide a valuable account of 'a writer so many-sided as to constitute a whole literature'. Here are poems from all periods of Goethe's creative life, including a complete version of the erotic *Roman Elegies*.

Hölderlin: *Poems and Fragments*

Michael Hamburger has been translating the poetry of Friedrich Hölderlin (1770–1843) for over half a century. This fourth edition contains the greater part of Hölderlin's odes in classical metre, the most characteristic of the later elegies, all the free-verse hymns (including many fragments of hymns drafted before the poet's withdrawal from society) as well as the second and third versions of his great tragedy *Der Tod des Empedokles*. It is likely to remain the standard bilingual edition of Hölderlin's poetry for many years.